The Selfish Truth

Every Decision Is Self-Serving, and That Is Perfectly Fine

Rob Gallant

Published 2026
ISBN: 979-8-9963374-7-7
Printed in the United States of America
First Edition

For everyone who has ever been called selfish,
and was probably just making the best decision available.

Contents

Page numbers update on final layout in Word.

Preface

This is a short book about a long misunderstanding.

The word "selfish" has been used as an insult for so long that we have nearly forgotten it could mean anything else. We wield it like an accusation. We shrink from it when it is aimed at us. We spend enormous energy defending ourselves against it, insisting to anyone who will listen that we are generous, considerate, and anything but selfish.

This book asks you to pause that defense for a moment.

What if the story we tell about selfishness is simply wrong? What if the behavior we call selfish is not a moral failure but a structural feature of how every human decision is made? And what if understanding that feature -- clearly and without the emotional baggage attached to it -- could actually help us treat each other better?

These are not rhetorical questions. They have answers, and the answers are found in evolutionary biology, behavioral science, and plain observation of how people make choices every single day. The framework offered in this book is not an excuse for bad behavior. It is an honest lens through which to understand behavior at all.

The argument is simple: every decision a person makes is, at its core, the option that person believed was best for themselves in that moment. That is what we will call the selfish principle. It does not mean people are cruel, calculating, or indifferent to others. It means that even our most generous, loving, and courageous acts are chosen because something in us recognizes them as the right choice. And the right choice is always, in one sense or another, the one that aligns with who we are and what we value.

Once you see it that way, the word "selfish" starts to lose its sting. And something more interesting takes its place.

Chapter 1

The Word That Makes Everyone Cringe

"It's challenging to learn something new, but more challenging to unlearn something that is no longer true."

Say the word "selfish" in a room full of people and watch what happens. Someone shifts in their seat. Someone else straightens up as if preparing a counterargument. A few people will glance around to see who is being accused. Almost no one sits comfortably with the word itself.

That discomfort is revealing. It tells us how deeply we have tied the concept of selfishness to moral failure. To be selfish, in the popular imagination, is to be a lesser person. It is the quality of someone who takes without giving, who advances without caring about the people left behind, who makes choices with a cold calculation that excludes everyone but themselves.

We teach our children to avoid it. We use it to explain villains in stories. We invoke it in arguments when we want to land a decisive blow. It is one of the most loaded words in the language, and that weight is almost entirely negative.

But here is the problem: the emotional charge around the word has made it nearly impossible to examine honestly. When a concept triggers defensiveness before analysis, we lose the ability to understand it. And if selfishness is as universal as this book will argue, then our failure to understand it clearly has real costs.

* * *

The Reflexive Denial

Almost universally, when people are described as selfish, the first response is denial. "I am not selfish." The denial is usually genuine. People do not believe themselves to be selfish because they carry an image of what selfishness looks like, and that image does not match what they see in the mirror.

The selfish person in the cultural imagination is the one who eats the last slice without asking, who cuts in line, who forgets birthdays, who uses friends for favors and disappears when they are needed in return. Most of us know people like this, at least occasionally. Most of us also know ourselves to be different, much of the time.

And yet we make decisions every day that prioritize our own interests, our own comfort, our own values, and our own vision of the future. We choose careers that align with what we want. We form relationships with people we enjoy. We spend money on things that matter to us. We volunteer for causes we believe in -- which are also causes we chose because we believe in them.

If all of those choices qualify as selfish, which this book will argue they do, then the cultural definition of selfishness is simply inadequate. It describes a narrow slice of a phenomenon far larger and more fundamental.

* * *

Taking the Emotion Out

The first task, then, is linguistic and psychological: we need to strip the word of its emotional charge long enough to examine what it actually describes.

This is harder than it sounds. Words carry accumulated meaning, and that accumulated meaning shapes how we think. Telling someone to take the emotion out of a word they have been taught to recoil from is a little like telling someone not to think of a pink elephant. The instruction creates the very problem it tries to solve.

> *"A mind is like a parachute. It doesn't work if it is not open."* -- Frank Zappa[1]

The approach here is not to argue that selfishness is good. It is to argue that selfishness, properly understood, is neither good nor bad. It is a description of how decisions are made, not a judgment about the quality of those decisions. Once we can hold it that way, we can start asking more useful questions: What makes some self-interested decisions beneficial for everyone involved, and what makes others destructive? How do two self-interested actors create either cooperation or conflict? What can we do to nudge the equation toward better outcomes?

These are questions worth asking. But we cannot ask them well if we are still flinching every time the word comes up.

So for the duration of this book, we will treat "selfish" as a neutral descriptor. It means: acting from a position of perceived self-interest. Nothing more, and nothing less.

---

[1]Frank Zappa, attributed. Widely cited in motivational and educational literature.

Chapter 2

Redefining the Word: What Selfish Really Means

> *"Every truth has two sides; it is as well to look at both before we commit ourselves to either."* -- Aesop[2]

Every definition carries a theory of human nature inside it. The dictionary tells us that selfish means "lacking consideration for others" or "concerned chiefly with one's own personal profit or pleasure." Both definitions presuppose that considering others and considering oneself are in opposition, and that choosing yourself means ignoring everyone else.

That is the theory of human nature embedded in the common definition of selfishness. And it is, as we will see, incomplete.

A Better Definition

Consider instead a functional definition: a decision is selfish when it reflects the decision-maker's best assessment of what serves their interests, values, and needs in that moment. Nothing in this definition implies that others are excluded. It simply says that the person making the decision is, inevitably, the person making it. Their perspective, their values, their understanding of the situation are what generate the choice.

Under this definition, the parent who stays up all night with a sick child is making a selfish decision. So is the surgeon who spends an extra hour ensuring a clean closure. So is the stranger who stops to help someone whose car has broken down on the highway. In each case, the person is choosing the action that aligns with who they are and what they value most.

---

[2]Aesop, Aesop's Fables, attributed c. 620-564 BCE.

This might seem to drain the word of any meaning. If everything is selfish, then nothing is. But that conclusion misses the point. The point is not that all actions are equivalent. It is that all actions originate from the same place: a human being choosing what they believe is the best available option, given their values and their perception of the situation.

* * *

The Moral Layer

The moral dimension of any given choice lies not in whether it is selfish, but in what values drive it. A person who values the wellbeing of others will make decisions that look generous, kind, and sacrificial. A person who values only their own immediate comfort will make decisions that look cruel, inconsiderate, or destructive. But both are acting from their own value system. Both are, in the sense used here, being selfish.

This reframe has an important consequence: it shifts the moral conversation away from whether someone is selfish, and toward what values they are expressing through their choices. That is a much more useful conversation. It asks people to examine their values rather than defending themselves against a label.

Consider a real-world example. Two people are asked to donate to a cause. One donates because they genuinely care about the cause and feel that contributing aligns with their deepest values. The other donates to look good in front of their peers, or to receive a tax benefit. We might judge the motivations differently. But in both cases, the person is doing what they believed was their best option given who they are and what they want. Both decisions are selfish. The difference lies in the values driving them, not in whether self-interest is present.

Selfishness is the mechanism. Values are the content. Understanding the mechanism clearly is what allows us to engage meaningfully with the content.

* * *

People Are Not Wired to Choose Badly

Here is one of the more counterintuitive claims in this book: people do not choose to make bad decisions. No one wakes up in the morning with the intention of making the worst possible choice. Every decision a person makes is, at the moment it is made, the option they believe is best for them.

This does not mean people always make good decisions. They make poor decisions constantly. They make decisions based on incomplete information, distorted thinking, short-term impulses that override long-term wellbeing, and all manner of cognitive bias. But even those flawed decisions are the best that person could see given their state of mind and knowledge at that moment.

The implication is important: when someone makes a decision that hurts others, the solution is rarely to accuse them of selfishness in the traditional sense. The more productive question is: what did they believe about the situation? What values were they expressing? What would it have taken for them to see more clearly?

> *"Never has anyone deliberately chosen a worse decision instead of the best one -- nonetheless, terrible things happen."*

This framing removes a certain comfortable simplicity from our moral judgments. We cannot simply write people off as selfish and walk away. We have to ask harder questions about values, perception, and context. That is more work. But it is also more honest.

Chapter 3

Written in Our DNA: The Biological Roots of Self-Interest

> *"It is not the strongest of the species that survive, but the one most responsive to change."* -- Charles Darwin[3]

If selfish decision-making feels universal, that is because it is. The tendency to prioritize one's own survival, reproduction, and wellbeing is not a cultural artifact or a personality flaw. It is one of the oldest and most deeply embedded features of biological life on earth.

The argument was made with extraordinary clarity and precision by Richard Dawkins in his landmark 1976 book, *The Selfish Gene.*[4] Dawkins proposed that the fundamental unit of natural selection is not the individual organism but the gene. Genes that promote the survival and reproduction of their carriers persist. Genes that do not, disappear. Over billions of years, this simple mechanism has produced organisms of stunning complexity, all of them shaped by the imperative to survive and reproduce.

The "selfish" in Dawkins's title refers to the gene, not the organism. Genes do not have intentions. They do not scheme or calculate. But they behave as if they do, because the ones that behave otherwise have long since ceased to exist. The result is organisms -- including human beings -- whose behavioral tendencies are fundamentally oriented around self-preservation and self-perpetuation.

---

[3]Charles Darwin, On the Origin of Species (London: John Murray, 1859).

[4]Richard Dawkins, The Selfish Gene (Oxford: Oxford University Press, 1976).

* * *

The Controversial but Necessary Idea

This idea has always generated resistance. The notion that human behavior is rooted in biological self-interest can feel like a reduction -- a dismissal of love, generosity, sacrifice, and all the qualities that make us proud to be human. The science communicators at Kurzgesagt explored this reaction directly in their video essay, "The Most Controversial Idea in Biology,"

[5] noting that people often hear the selfish gene hypothesis as an argument that humans are fundamentally bad. That is not what the science says.

What the science says is that self-interest is built into the machinery of life. But that machinery produces remarkable outputs. It produces parents who sacrifice sleep, comfort, and career for their children. It produces soldiers who lay down their lives for their comrades. It produces scientists who give their discoveries freely to the world. None of these behaviors contradict the selfish gene. They are among its most spectacular expressions.

> *"People acting in their own self-interest is the fuel for discovery, innovation, and prosperity."* -- John Stossel[6]

The reason is kin selection and reciprocal altruism. Protecting your children is self-interest in genetic terms. Helping your community creates a social environment that benefits you in return. Even the most generous-seeming behavior, examined closely, has a logic that connects it to the interests of the person performing it. That connection is not a scandal. It is the engine of social life.

---

[5]Kurzgesagt, "The Most Controversial Idea in Biology," YouTube, 2021.

[6]John Stossel, Give Me a Break (New York: HarperCollins, 2004).

* * *

The Survival Logic

At its most basic level, the biological need to survive is the original selfish impulse. The organism that does not prioritize its own survival does not live long enough to pass anything on. Every living thing that exists today is the descendant of a long line of organisms that found food before they starved, avoided predators before they were caught, and reproduced before they died.

In humans, this survival logic does not operate only at the level of food and physical safety. We have extended it into territory that no other species occupies: social status, emotional wellbeing, meaning, legacy, and identity. We are selfish about our reputations. We are selfish about our beliefs. We are selfish about the futures we imagine for ourselves and our families.

That extension is what makes human selfishness so rich and so complicated. We are not just trying to survive the next winter. We are trying to build a life that feels worth living, and we bring the same biological imperative to that project that our ancestors brought to the hunt.

> *"The unexamined life is not worth living."* --
> Socrates

Understanding the biological foundation of self-interest is not an invitation to surrender to our lowest impulses. It is an invitation to understand where our impulses come from, so that we can engage with them honestly and direct them wisely.

Chapter 4

The Architecture of Every Decision

"We can't control the outcome. We can't control the decisions. At best, we can influence the choice."

Every decision follows the same basic architecture. There is a person with needs, values, and a perception of the world. There is a set of available options, as that person understands them. And there is a choice -- which is always the option that person believes, in that moment, best serves their interests and values.

This architecture is not peculiar to any culture, personality type, or economic situation. It describes how choices are made across the entire range of human experience, from the trivial (which coffee to order) to the profound (whether to stay in a struggling relationship or leave). In every case, the person chooses what seems best to them.

Defining Best

The slipperiness in this framework is the word "best." What counts as best varies enormously from person to person and situation to situation. For one person, the best decision is the one that maximizes financial security. For another, it is the one that maintains a valued relationship. For a third, it is the one that feels morally correct even at personal cost. For a fourth, it is the one that creates the least immediate discomfort, regardless of long-term consequences.

None of these criteria is objectively correct. But in every case, the person is using their version of "best" to navigate toward a choice. And in every case, the choice they make is, at minimum, the one they could not immediately identify a better alternative to.

"The best decision is better than a good one, a good one is better than indecision, and indecision is better than no decision at all."

This is why the claim that people choose badly so often is true and yet still compatible with the principle that everyone makes the best decision available. Making the best decision available does not require access to perfect information, a fully rational mind, or a clear view of long-term consequences. It only requires that in this moment, with what the person knows and believes and feels, the choice they made was the one they could not easily improve upon.

* * *

The Decision Pyramid

Not all decisions carry equal weight -- and not all are made with the same quality of thought. The Decision Pyramid maps the spectrum from the best possible choice down to the worst: no decision at all. Understanding where your decision lands on this pyramid is the first step toward consistently making better ones.

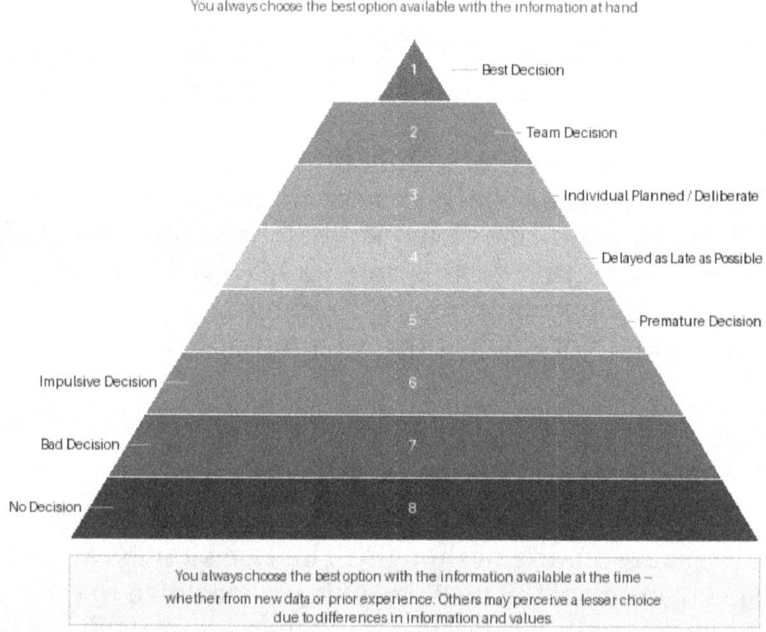

Figure 4.1 -- The Decision Pyramid

1. **Best Decision:** Optimal -- drawn from full context, aligned values, and complete available information.
2. **Team Decision:** Collective input improves the outcome. Multiple perspectives reduce blind spots.
3. **Individual Planned / Deliberate Decision:** Thoughtful, solo analysis with adequate time and information.
4. **Delayed as Late as Possible:** Waiting for more information when time permits. Not avoidance -- strategy.
5. **Premature Decision:** Decided before sufficient information was gathered. Risk increases.
6. **Impulsive Decision:** Reactive. Emotion or urgency overrides analysis.

7. **Bad Decision:** A choice made with available information that, in hindsight, was the wrong call.
8. **No Decision:** The worst outcome. Inaction is itself a decision -- one that forfeits control.

Three principles govern every level of this pyramid.

First: you always choose the best option with the information you have available at the time. That information can be new data you just received or hard-won knowledge drawn from experience. Neither is inherently superior -- both are legitimate inputs to a sound decision.

Second: you will never knowingly choose a lesser option. This is not optimism. It is the structural reality of how decisions work. The moment a person identifies a better option, that becomes the option they choose. What appears to be a bad decision from the outside is almost always the best that person could see from the inside.

Third: others may perceive that you chose a lesser option. That perception is real, and it matters. But it arises not because you failed to choose well -- it arises because others hold different information or different values. The gap between your decision and their expectation is an information gap, not a character flaw.

This is why the pyramid matters. It is not a ranking of people. It is a ranking of decision conditions. Move the conditions upward -- add information, involve the right people, allow adequate time -- and the quality of decisions follows.

* * *

The Role of Values

Values are the lenses through which options are evaluated. Two people facing identical circumstances may make entirely different choices because they hold different values, not because one of them is making a mistake.

Imagine two colleagues offered a promotion that requires frequent travel. One accepts enthusiastically because they value career advancement and adventure. The other declines because they value presence at home with young children. Both are making the best decision for themselves. Both are being selfish in the functional sense of acting on their own values. Neither is wrong.

Where value systems align, decisions tend to be mutually reinforcing. Where they diverge, decisions create friction. This is the key to understanding conflict, which Chapter 6 will examine directly.

> *"Opinions are based on today; be prepared to adjust them tomorrow."*

For now, the critical point is this: the content of our values shapes the quality of our decisions, but the mechanism of decision-making is the same for everyone. All decisions flow from perceived self-interest, filtered through the decision-maker's values and understanding. That is the architecture. Everything else is detail.

* * *

The Illusion of Objectivity

We tend to believe we make decisions objectively, weighing evidence and arriving at rational conclusions. Research in behavioral economics and cognitive psychology has spent decades dismantling this belief. We are subject to confirmation bias, availability heuristics, loss aversion, anchoring effects, and dozens of other systematic distortions that shape our decisions without our awareness.

More relevant to this discussion: we tend to believe that our values are simply correct, while others' values are distorted by self-interest. We see our own self-interest as reasonable and justified. We see others' self-interest as selfish in the pejorative sense.

This double standard is itself a form of self-interest. It protects our sense of ourselves as reasonable, moral people. And it is nearly universal. Understanding that both parties in any disagreement are operating from perceived self-interest -- filtered through values -- is the first step toward genuinely productive engagement.

Chapter 5

When Selfish Meets Selfish: The Two-Actor Equation

> *"Improving your world starts with improving someone else's world."* -- Unknown

Now we come to the genuinely interesting part. A single person making decisions in isolation is one thing. But most decisions are not made in isolation. They are made in the presence of, and in response to, other people who are also making decisions from their own perceived self-interest.

What happens when two selfish actors meet?

The answer, perhaps surprisingly, is often something good. In fact, the mutual exchange of two parties each pursuing their own interests is the basis of trade, cooperation, friendship, and society itself. When the self-interests of two people are aligned, or when pursuing one's interest requires attending to the other's, the result can be powerfully positive for both.

The Market as a Model

The simplest illustration is an economic exchange. A seller wants to receive money. A buyer wants to receive a product or service. Neither is primarily motivated by the other's wellbeing. Yet the transaction serves both parties. The seller's interest in profit and the buyer's interest in value create, between them, an exchange that neither could achieve alone.

This is the fundamental insight of free market economics, and while markets can fail in important ways, the basic dynamic is real: mutual self-interest, when properly structured, produces mutual benefit. The mechanism is not charity or altruism. It is the alignment of selfish interests.

"The best solutions include we, not just me."

The same logic applies far beyond commerce. Two friends who enjoy each other's company meet regularly because each enjoys the other's presence. Neither is being selflessly generous with their time. Each is choosing to spend time in a way they find rewarding. The friendship flourishes because their self-interests are compatible.

A team working on a project can achieve remarkable things when each member's interest in doing good work, in being recognized, and in belonging to something meaningful all point in the same direction. The team's success is not the product of individual selflessness. It is the product of individual self-interest, structured so that helping the team is also helping oneself.

* * *

The Compound Effect of Aligned Self-Interest

When we understand this dynamic, the question of how to build good teams, good relationships, and good organizations becomes clearer. The goal is not to eliminate self-interest but to align it. Structure things so that what is good for one actor is also good for the others. Create environments where helping your colleagues advances your own standing. Build relationships where treating the other person well is also the most rewarding experience for you.

> *"A sign of a good leader is not how many followers they have, but how many leaders they create."* -- Unknown

This is what great leadership does. It does not ask people to be selfless. It builds situations in which people's natural self-interest leads them toward shared goals. The leader who takes this seriously stops trying to overcome human nature and starts working with it.

The same applies in any close relationship. Partners who understand that the other's self-interest is a feature rather than a threat can build something far more durable than those who expect constant selflessness. Each party attending to their own genuine needs and values, in a context where doing so also supports the other, creates a relationship that neither could maintain alone.

* * *

When Both Actors Decide, Good Things Often Follow

The broader claim here is important enough to state plainly: when two actors each bring their own self-interested decision to a shared situation, and when both decisions are respected, the outcome tends to be positive. A negotiation where both parties are honest about their interests usually arrives at a better agreement than one where one party pretends to be indifferent to outcome. A relationship where both people can name what they need is more stable than one where one person silently sacrifices.

> *"If you want to go fast, go alone. If you want to go far, go together."* -- African Proverb

The two-actor model of mutual self-interest is, at its best, an engine of human cooperation. The problem arises not when two people are both self-interested, but when their self-interests pull in incompatible directions. That is the subject of the next chapter.

Chapter 6

The Friction Point: When Decisions Collide

> *"If an argument lasts more than five minutes, then both sides are wrong."* -- Neil deGrasse Tyson[7]

Not all meetings of two self-interested actors go smoothly. When the self-interest of one person points in one direction and the self-interest of another points in the opposite direction, friction is the inevitable result. And this friction, rather than evidence that one party is selfish in the negative sense, is simply the natural consequence of two legitimate interests in conflict.

Understanding this changes how we approach conflict. If conflict arises because one person is selfish and the other is not, then the solution is for the selfish party to stop being selfish. That framing places blame and demands moral reform. It rarely works. But if conflict arises because two self-interested parties have incompatible goals, then the question is entirely different: how can the situation be restructured so that both parties' interests are served?

The Take-and-Keep Dynamic

Consider the most common form of interpersonal friction. Person A wants something. Person B has it, or has what is needed to provide it. Person A's selfish decision is to take, acquire, or receive. Person B's selfish decision is to keep, protect, or withhold. Both decisions are equally selfish in the functional sense. But the resulting dynamic is the one that

---

[7]Neil deGrasse Tyson, attributed. StarTalk podcast and public lectures.

popular culture calls selfishness: one party is trying to take what the other wants to keep.

This imbalance is the origin of most conflict. It does not arise because one party is fundamentally better or worse than the other. It arises because their interests, at this particular moment, are pointed in opposite directions. The parent who wants their teenager home by ten and the teenager who wants to stay until midnight are both acting selfishly. The employer who wants more work for less pay and the employee who wants more pay for less work are both acting selfishly. The friction between them is not a moral problem. It is a coordination problem.

"Discourse is the debate where everyone wins."

When we recognize conflict as a coordination problem rather than a moral one, new solutions become available. Instead of asking who is right and who is selfish, we can ask: what would it take for both parties to walk away satisfied? What interests, if we look beneath the stated positions, might actually be compatible? What creative arrangement might serve both parties' genuine needs?

* * *

The One-Actor Imbalance

The situation becomes categorically different when only one party is making a fully self-interested decision. Consider an exchange in which one party takes and the other does not consciously choose to give. In ordinary commerce, the seller decides to sell and the buyer decides to buy. Both parties' self-interest is engaged. But if one party takes without the other's decision being involved, the dynamic changes.

This is the scenario that most closely matches what we ordinarily call selfish in the negative sense: one person's decision is active and self-serving, while the other person's situation is altered without their meaningful participation in the decision. The friction this creates is justified. It is not merely a coordination problem. It is a violation of the reciprocal self-interest that makes cooperation possible.

The solution is not to eliminate self-interest but to restore reciprocity. Both parties must be in a position where their decisions matter, where their interests are visible, and where the outcome reflects both actors rather than just one.

* * *

Good People, Difficult Outcomes

One of the most important things to grasp about the friction point is that it does not require bad intentions. Ordinary people, pursuing entirely reasonable goals, create real harm in each other's lives through the collision of incompatible self-interests. This is not because they are selfish in the pejorative sense. It is because self-interest, even when it is well-intentioned and value-driven, can still conflict with others' equally well-intentioned and value-driven self-interest.

> *"Nobody drives to work in a rage set on screwing things up -- nonetheless, things get screwed up."*

Holding this truth does not remove accountability. People whose decisions harm others bear responsibility for that harm, whether or not they intended it. But it does suggest that the path forward lies not in demanding that people stop being self-interested, which is impossible, but in creating the conditions under which their self-interest and others' self-interest are more likely to point in compatible directions.

Chapter 7

The Dog Dilemma: A Practical Illustration

"You can't connect the dots looking forward, only backward." -- Steve Jobs[8]

Abstract arguments are easier to understand when they are grounded in a specific situation. So consider this: you have a dog. You have an opportunity to travel for work, a trip that could advance your career and that you genuinely want to take. But the dog cannot travel with you. You have three options.

First, you hire a sitter. Second, you fly and leave the dog unattended, perhaps with a neighbor checking in intermittently. Third, you stay home entirely and forgo the trip.

Every single one of these options is selfish. All three represent your best assessment of what serves your interests, values, and sense of responsibility in this situation. And tracing the self-interest in each one illuminates the full texture of the framework.

Option One: The Sitter

Hiring a sitter is the option that best aligns two things you value: the professional opportunity and the wellbeing of your dog. The money spent on the sitter is a price you pay willingly because the alternative -- worrying about the dog for the entire trip, or feeling guilty, or coming home to an unhappy animal -- would diminish the value of the trip. You hire the sitter because doing so is the best available version of the

---

[8] Steve Jobs, Stanford University Commencement Address, June 12, 2005.

situation for you. It happens to also be good for the dog, but that is a consequence of your self-interest rather than a departure from it.

This is the two-actor scenario working well. Your interest in taking the trip and the dog's interest in being cared for are both served by the same decision. The sitter's interest in earning income is also served. Three sets of self-interest align, and the outcome is good for everyone.

* * *

Option Two: Flying and Leaving

Flying and leaving the dog without proper care is also self-interested, but it is self-interest in a narrower form. You have prioritized the professional and personal value of the trip above the dog's wellbeing. This is a legitimate choice in the sense that you are making the decision that best serves your interests as you understand them in this moment. But it creates the friction dynamic discussed in the previous chapter. The dog's interest in care and company is not part of the equation, because the dog cannot participate in the decision.

This is the one-actor imbalance. Your decision is fully self-interested and active. The dog's situation changes without its meaningful input. Whether this is a morally good decision depends on your values and the actual consequences for the dog. But structurally, it mirrors every situation in which one party's self-interest is fully expressed and another party's is not.

> *"Always ask: is it legal, ethical, and moral? If the answer is no, make another choice."*

Option Three: Staying Home

Staying home is, again, a selfish decision. You have decided that the guilt of leaving the dog, or the disruption to its routine, or your own sense of responsibility, outweighs the value of the professional opportunity. You are not being noble. You are being honest about what matters most to you. The calculation came out differently than it would for someone else, and so the decision is different.

This is not self-sacrifice. It is self-knowledge. You know yourself well enough to understand that going on the trip while worrying about the dog, or feeling guilty, would hollow out the experience. Staying home is what keeps your inner world intact. That is self-interest, expressed through a clear-eyed assessment of what you value.

* * *

What the Scenario Teaches

The dog dilemma makes visible what abstract argument sometimes obscures: every option in a real-world decision carries self-interest, even the one that looks most selfless. The parent who stays home with the sick child is not noble in a way that defies self-interest. They are expressing a value system in which that child's wellbeing is integral to their own.

> *"Everything is about perspective. If you find yourself with a stick in your eye, be thankful you don't have a stick in the other eye."*

What changes between the options is not whether self-interest is present but what values are shaping it and whose interests are accounted for in the decision. The more parties whose interests are included, the better the outcome tends to be for everyone. The more the decision narrows to a single party's immediate benefit, the more likely it is to create the friction we described in the previous chapter.

The dog cannot advocate for itself in human terms. But the dog's wellbeing is a real consideration that a thoughtful person includes in their self-interest, because their values extend to it. That extension of self-interest to include others is the defining feature of ethical behavior. It is not the absence of self-interest. It is the expansion of it.

Chapter 8

Making Peace With Our Nature

"When we strive to become better than we are, everything around us becomes better too." -- Paulo Coelho

We began with a word that makes people cringe. We end with a suggestion: what if that cringe has been holding us back?

The case made in this book is not a defense of cruelty, greed, or indifference to others. It is an argument for honest engagement with the actual mechanics of human decision-making. Every person who has ever been called selfish was, at that moment, doing exactly what every human being does: choosing the option they believed was best for them. The quality of that choice, and whether it honored or damaged the people around them, depended on their values -- not on whether self-interest was present.

Self-interest is always present. It is built into the biology. It is the operating system. The question is never whether someone is being selfish. The question is always what values are running on top of that operating system.

The Better Conversation

When we stop accusing each other of selfishness and start asking about values, the quality of our interactions improves. "You are being selfish" closes a conversation. "What are you trying to protect here?" opens one. The first statement assumes bad character. The second assumes a human being with legitimate interests that, for some reason, have ended up in conflict with yours.

This is not a naive approach. It does not require you to agree with the other person or to excuse harm. It requires only that you engage with what is actually happening: two self-interested actors whose interests have, in this moment, come into conflict. That conflict can often be resolved. It almost never can be resolved by insisting that the other person stop being what they inescapably are.

> *"Do the right thing, be kind, and the rest will fall into place."*

* * *

Expanding the Circle

Perhaps the most useful reframe this book can offer is this: the most admirable human behavior is not the absence of self-interest but the expansion of it. People who genuinely care about others do not stop caring about themselves. They have simply built a self that includes others in its circle of concern. Their wellbeing is genuinely entangled with the wellbeing of those around them, so that helping others is, for them, genuinely self-interested.

This is what parents feel for children. What lifelong partners feel for each other. What the best leaders feel for the people they serve. Their self-interest is broad enough to encompass people beyond themselves, which means that acting on self-interest leads to behavior we recognize as generous, courageous, and good.

> *"I measure my own success by how successful those are that I influence."* -- Adapted from Maria Shi

Cultivating that kind of expanded self-interest is a worthy life project. It does not require denying your nature. It requires developing it. The person who cares about strangers is not less selfish than the person who does not. They have simply built a more expansive self.

* * *

A Final Word on the Word

Language matters. The word “selfish” has been weaponized so thoroughly that it is hard to reclaim. This book does not ask you to walk around calling yourself selfish in casual conversation. It asks you to understand the concept clearly enough that the accusation loses its power.

When someone calls you selfish, you can now hear that as: “Your decision serves your interests in a way that conflicts with mine, and I have not been able to see your perspective clearly enough to understand why.” That is the beginning of a more productive conversation.

And when you are tempted to call someone else selfish, you can catch yourself and ask instead: what are they trying to protect? What values are they expressing? How can we find an arrangement where both our sets of self-interest can be honored?

> *“Life isn’t about finding yourself. Life is about creating yourself.”* -- George Bernard Shaw[9]

We are all selfish. We have always been. The goal is not to stop being selfish. The goal is to become the kind of person whose self-interest leads toward something worth building.

---

[9] George Bernard Shaw, Back to Methuselah (London: Constable, 1921), Preface.

References

Primary Sources

Dawkins, Richard. The Selfish Gene. Oxford: Oxford University Press, 1976. Fortieth anniversary edition.

Darwin, Charles. On the Origin of Species by Means of Natural Selection. London: John Murray, 1859.

Kurzgesagt. "The Most Controversial Idea in Biology." YouTube, 2021.

Further Reading

Aesop. Aesop's Fables. Various translators and editions. Attributed c. 620-564 BCE.

Emerson, Ralph Waldo. "Success." In The Complete Works of Ralph Waldo Emerson. Boston: Houghton Mifflin, 1904.

Kahneman, Daniel. Thinking, Fast and Slow. New York: Farrar, Straus and Giroux, 2011.

Sinek, Simon. Start With Why. New York: Portfolio/Penguin, 2009.

Shaw, George Bernard. Back to Methuselah. London: Constable and Company, 1921.

Stossel, John. Give Me a Break. New York: HarperCollins, 2004.

Wilson, Edward O. The Social Conquest of Earth. New York: Liveright, 2012.

www.ingramcontent.com/pod-product-compliance
Lightning Source LLC
LaVergne TN
LVHW010841120826
845149LV00020B/3486

* 9 7 9 8 9 9 6 3 3 7 4 7 7 *